Marketing Musts

Dave Hughes

This book is dedicated to my wife Chris, who has stood behind me through thick and thin. Always and forever, baby.

I'd also like to dedicate this book to my two sons, Ryan and Drake; Ryan for the inspiration of his unceasing thought processes on everything around him (and good ideas, too), and Drake for two things: providing the cover photo when he was still in daycare, and for a never-ending daily question that made this book possible: "Did you finish your book yet, Daddy?"

If you have any questions (or just need a hand), visit Dave Hughes Consulting on the web:

http://davehughesconsulting.com

You'll find free gifts, a blog full of more marketing tips and information, and more information on how Dave Hughes Consulting can help increase your profits.

Would you like your revenue to increase by 20% in the next 60 days?

http://davehughesconsulting.com

(If you said "no" to that question, nice job! You're the first business owner I've found that had all the revenue he wanted!)

Table of Contents

- **Michael Jordan** was cut from his high school basketball team.

- **Henry Ford** went bankrupt five times before he became a success in automobile manufacturing.

- **Walt Disney** was fired by a newspaper editor because he "lacked imagination."

- In 1954, the manager of the Grand Ole Opry fired **Elvis Presley** after one performance, telling him "You ain't goin' nowhere, son. You ought to go back to drivin' a truck."

It's not whether or not you're good...it's whether or not you can convince *everyone else* you are.

Owning and operating a business is hard.

If you've never done it, chances are you've never even thought about it. And even when you do take the plunge, it seems like a million things pop up that you never saw coming. At times, it can turn into a "take care of the most important emergency first" battle that never seems to end.

One part of owning a business that many seem to put on the back burner is marketing. Don't get me wrong; most business owners advertise, but advertising is a marketing *tool*, not marketing. And just like any other tool, it isn't very effective if it isn't used correctly, and with the other tools needed to complete the job.

In this book, I outline the ten things you should keep

in mind when thinking about marketing your business. These vary in importance from "This is very important" to "This is incredibly important" to *"Holy cow! I've got to get this done ASAP!"* The "Holy Cow!" variety is what you'll find as step number two. If it's that important, Dave, why is it at number two?

Simple. Until you read and fully understand step one, step two isn't going to happen.

Effective marketing isn't a mystical art, nor is it a hard science full of math. It's worse...effective marketing is a combination of the two. However, the good news is, it *can* be learned.

Here's to millions!

When Bell telephone was struggling to get started, its owners offered all their rights to Western Union for $100,000. The offer was disdainfully rejected with the pronouncement, "What use could this company make of an electrical toy."

<u>Chapter One:</u>
You Are *NOT* Your Target Market

Before we get into the nuts and bolts of improving

your marketing efforts, we first have to deal with a very

common problem among business owners.

Not many people run a business just because it's

"something to do"...in most cases, it's a passion. Your business

may be a dream you had that you have finally made true, a

family legacy that you take pride in and want to see have

continued success, or a "happy accident" that you just stumbled

upon that gave you the opportunity to stop working for

someone else.

In every single one of those cases, it guarantees one thing; you are not your target market, period.

I know, I know..."But Dave, I got into this because it was something I used or believed in!" I have no doubt that's true, nor do I doubt that your business is providing goods or services that people want and need. However, the potential customers you're trying to convince of that are not asking the same questions you are. In fact, chances are you're not asking *any* questions at *all*. See if anything on this list sounds familiar:

- I've got the best customer service around; why wouldn't anyone want to do business with me?

- I've got the best product around; why wouldn't anyone want to do business with me?

- I do a better job than anyone else around; why wouldn't anyone want to do business with me?

- Why would anyone have any questions? It's obvious that I have what people need at a great price!

You may not have ever said those words out loud, but the real question you need to answer for yourself is "Do I have those opinions, or anything close to them?" If so, then you have no idea how to address your potential customers' concerns, for a very good reason:

When you are offering something you truly believe in, something that you know to the bottom of your soul is the absolute best thing a person could spend their money on in your industry, you have a hard time imagining what questions anyone *could* possibly have.

I mean, it's so obvious, right? Anyone with "walking around sense" can see that you've got the best product...why don't *they* see it?

It's hard to market a business you're passionate about for the same reason that no one thinks your kids (or grandkids) are nearly as cute as you do.

You love those kids with all your heart; they might make you mad some days, they may aggravate you at times, and there are days when you wonder if it wouldn't have been better to just get a dog, but in the end those are your babies, and their faults are never as obvious to you as they are to others.

Replace the word "kids" with the word "business" in that sentence, and clean up the pronouns, etc. to fit. Here, I'll do it for you:

You love that business with all your heart; it might make you mad some days, it may aggravate you at times, and there are days when you wonder if it wouldn't have been better to just get a hobby, but in the end that business is your baby, and its faults are never as obvious to you as they are to others.

This can lead to a real problem when it comes time to market your business effectively. If you're blind to the problems your baby has, then you're not going to even know there is something that *needs* fixing, much less *how* to fix it. And to top that off, when someone tells you what they perceive to be the problems with your baby, it'll just make you mad that they dare to insist that your precious little snowflake is anything other than perfect.

Admit it; when someone points out a fault with your

business, even if they're perfectly correct...it irritates you, at

least a little. What most people fail to realize is that irritation is

great, as long as you use it to your advantage.

If you want to know the absolute worst about your

kids, ask someone that can't stand you. No, really. If they've

spent any amount of time around your offspring, they will run

down a laundry list of real and perceived faults that will make

your hair curl. Of course, you'll take this with a huge grain of

salt, but if the truth be told...there probably *is* some truth buried

in there.

Now, ask your mom about your kids. She may

(emphasis on "may") list a few faults, but it'll be a completely

different list than the first one if she does; shorter, nicer and

more constructive. It's also quite possible that she won't have a bad word to say about her precious grandchildren, and let's face it, no one's perfect.

You *trust* the second list, but the first list would be much more *useful* for you. The short form of this is "Don't ask your mama how your business is doing," because you're most likely not going to get anything useful out of it.

If you realize that you're too close to your business emotionally to see objectively what could be limiting your success (which is a fancy way of saying "You're not your target market"), then congratulations! That's a big step for anyone to take. What is just as important, though, is realizing what to do about it.

Decca Records turned down a recording contract with the Beatles with the unprophetic evaluation, "We don't like their sound. Groups of guitars are on their way out." After Decca rejected the Beatles, Columbia records followed suit.

<u>Chapter Two:</u>
What's Your USP?

If you have no idea what I'm talking about, then I'm about to introduce a serious shift in the way you look at your business.

USP stands for "Unique Selling Proposition," and if you don't have one you could be in *serious* trouble. The good news is, you most likely have one and don't even know it.

A USP tells everyone that sees or hears it one thing; what you offer that no one else in your line of business offers. Period. It's not a catchy slogan (although it can be). It's not a snappy line to throw out at parties (although it can be). It's not your entire marketing campaign (although it is the single most important thing to have for one). Having said that, what's *your* USP? What can you say about your business that none of your competitors can *truthfully* say about theirs?

Whatever your USP is, it should be front and center in all of your marketing efforts...no excuses, no exceptions. The interesting thing is just how hard it can be to figure out what your USP actually *is*. Here's a list of some things that business owners think are their USP, even though they're *not*:

Customer Service – Unless you're in a business where all the competition has a reputation for throwing people out of their door or cursing at them when they call to make a purchase, this isn't a USP. Look around at your competitors; if they answer their phones at least semi-promptly, welcome

customers through the door with a smile and help them with

their problems, then "good customer service" isn't unique. It's

also not a "selling proposition"; despite what many business

owners think. Customer service doesn't close many sales; a *lack*

of it will *lose* you a good bit of business, but that's because it's

expected. And something that's expected of everyone isn't going

to bring new business through the door, for the same reason that

no one's surprised when they go to the grocery store to get milk

and it's there. Now, if they are *out* of milk, *then* it makes a

difference, but not if the customer gets what they expect. Stop

patting yourself on the back and keep digging for your USP.

Widest Selection – Does your area have the internet?

Then guess what? You don't have the "widest selection" of your products...that's in your customers' computer rooms, from all over the world. That's not to say that your selection isn't fantastic, nor does it mean that having the widest selection around won't bring customers to your business, but it is a claim that's going to be hard to back up these days.

Lowest Prices – This can be part of a good USP, but it has to be true. Getting "close" doesn't cut it. Undercutting by just a cent or two won't cut it. It would have to be a "impact" price difference; a large enough savings for a customer to justify making the trip to your business instead of where they were going already. "Drive a little, save a lot!" is a slogan used by some to help illustrate that, but that is not a USP...it's a *slogan*. Remember, your USP should be something that no one else can say about their business.

Twenty years combined experience – Or thirty, or

seventy-five, or eleventy-bajillion; the number makes no

difference, and neither does this claim in the eyes of your

potential customers. Let's look at that example, "twenty years

combined experience"; so, you have twenty employees that

have been doing it a year each? Ten employees with two years'

each? Or one grizzled vet in the back? It's a phrase that sounds

great to a business owner, but ultimately doesn't mean much to

potential customers that hear it. Again, this is an

expectation...for most types of business, not many people walk

in thinking to themselves "Boy, I hope they're experienced at

this!" The service industry can make a case for this type of

claim, but only to a certain point. When it gets right down to it,

potential customers don't want to know how long you've been

doing things for other people...they want to know what you're going to do for *them*.

Convenient Location – This is not the selling point you think it is. Your location is important, but primarily for walk-in business or impulse purchases. The importance of this one varies depending on what kind of business you have; no one cares where the plumber's office is located...the leaky pipe is at *their* house. (I knew a plumber that actually used his convenient location in his marketing, to no effect.) If you sell auto parts, it might have a bit more relevance, but not as much as you think. Marketing isn't making someone realize you're easy to get to, it's making them realize that it doesn't matter where you're at, you're the only one that can help them fulfill their need or desire.

So, what *does* make up a good USP? It's deceptively simple; a good USP will be:

- Completely true.

- Something that shows the value you give your customers, answering their unspoken question "What's in it for me?"

- Something that *none* of your competitors can truthfully say about themselves.

And that's it. Any more is just filler, which won't help convince anyone to give you their money. Any less, and it won't be *enough* to convince anyone.

There have been entire books written about how to find your USP, and we obviously can't cover the entire process here. However, there is one thing to keep in mind when trying to find your USP...the most important part; answer this question correctly and completely, and you'll be well on your way to finding yours:

What do you offer than no one else does in your market?

Remember, it has to be something that none of your competitors offer...the only place that someone can get this is with you. And it has to be something that is a benefit to a potential customer, not a feature of your business. "Largest selection in the area" is a feature, while "You'll never have to drive all over town to find what you need if you come here first, we guarantee it!" is a benefit.

Don't be surprised if it's harder than it looks to find this. Again, outside help is invaluable. If you think you've created the perfect USP for your business, bounce it off a few people you trust and ask them to poke as many holes in it as they can.

This boils down to one simple concept...you may think you know what's important to your customers about your business, but you probably have a completely different idea than they do. If you ever hear a customer say "I always come here, because it's the only place I can _____!", you just found a fantastic starting point for your USP.

"The more you like yourself, the less you are like anyone else, which makes you unique." -Walt Disney

Chapter Three:
Going up! The Elevator Pitch

"Okay, Dave...now you're just making things up." No, not at all. Let's play pretend for a minute, shall we?

You step onto an elevator, headed for an appointment on the tenth floor. You step inside and push the button labeled "10". Just as the door starts to close, you see someone hurrying across the lobby, saying "Hold the elevator, please!"

Being a nice person, you hold the door open until they get on, and then let it close. "What floor," you say, ready to push the button for them. "Tenth, please," he says, following with "Oh! We're headed to the same place. Great!"

The door closes, and the elevator starts to rise. Unlike most people in an elevator, however, this guy's a talker. "Whattya do?" he asks.

You've got to tell him what you do in such a way that he's interested, and his interest is captured to such a point that he wants to find out more, and would even be interested in doing business with you.

And you have to do it before the elevator door opens on the tenth floor.

That is an "elevator pitch". A short, to-the-point description of what you do that captures someone's attention and practically forces them to find out more. As you can imagine, "I'm a plumber" won't quite do it. You need to have your on the tip of your tongue, ready to pop out at every appropriate moment.

Finding your USP makes developing an elevator pitch a *lot* easier. However, your USP is not necessarily your elevator pitch. Let's look at some examples:

"I'm a plumber." is not an effective elevator pitch, while "I handle every pipe leak, faucet drip or plumbing installation for this entire area, with the only 100% satisfaction guarantee in the plumbing business around here. I'm the guy people call when no one else can help." is.

"I sell insurance." will quite possibly prompt a yawn from your audience, while "I'm a financial security guard. I protect people from losing everything they own just because they had some bad luck." is better, but not perfect.

This is the problem with "sample" elevator pitches; it has

to be something that you "own", factually *and* emotionally.

There is no magic book of elevator pitches, any more than there

is a "Big Book of USP's" floating around out there; your

elevator pitch should be unique to *your* business and

personality. It has to be something that is said with your

"voice"; it has to sound natural when you say it, and more

importantly...you have to believe it. If *you* don't, no one *else*

will, either.

To craft an elevator pitch for yourself, remember to think

outside of the box. Don't tell people what you do, tell them

what you do for people just like them. Don't give them a "career

label"...which one would you want to hear more about, a

"doctor" or someone who says "I've saved 232 lives so far this

year"?

"Never assume the obvious is true."
-William Safire

Chapter Four:
When you assume, you make...

...a big mistake.

Every business owner thinks they know what their customers are looking for. And guess what? Uncle Dave is going to give you this one...I have no doubt you *do* know what your customers want, and do your best to provide exactly that.

Where you can go wrong is assuming what your customers, both potential and current, actually know about what your business provides. At every step of your marketing, you...must...show...them.

Notice I didn't say "you must *tell* them." That is a different (and much less effective) thing.

If your best friend in the world told you that he had made friends with a five-armed alien from Venus called "Monkeyspit," what would your level of belief be? How much would you believe them if they told you the same thing, and then said "He's here visiting, let me introduce you. Hey, Monkeyspit!" and out walked a five-armed alien from Venus who croaked out "Nice to meet you, I've heard a lot about you."?

That's a fairly extreme example (unless you actually have a friend from Venus; if you do, I'd love an introduction myself), but the principle still holds true. Don't tell people what you do, **show them**. This doesn't necessarily mean with pictures...the words you use can paint a vivid picture. It's example time again!

Tell them: "We've been in the auto repair business since 1902, and our staff has over 80 years' experience!"

Show **them:** "In 1902, we fixed Robert McGee's wagon, and didn't even wake his horse up. In 1941, we got his son's family automobile running like it was brand-new. In 1976, we serviced Robert's granddaughter's car before she headed off to college. And in 2001, we got his great-grandson back up and running the roads after his fender-bender. We don't fix cars...we get generations where they need to go safely."

Yes, the "show them" example is longer by quite a bit, but guess what? The first version tells them what you do, while the second one shows them how you can become a part of the family. Let's try another, this time keeping the length roughly the same:

Tell them: "We provide a full range of insurance coverage, with a life, health, auto or home policy tailored to fit your needs."

***Show* them:** "With the new baby finally here, Tom was looking for the most unusual insurance requirements in a lot of different areas. We said "No problem.""

Don't *tell* your customers what you do, *show* them why it matters to them. And you must show them *everything*. Don't assume a potential customer will realize that your 100+ years of business experience makes you the obvious choice, show them why. Don't assume the fact that you have a ton of different policies and deductibles will make you the "go-to" agency in town, show them why that wide selection actually *matters* to them, and show them how it will make a difference in their lives.

In a very specialized way, customers are stupid.

I'll let you catch your breath for a minute; you've probably muttered that to yourself before, but can't believe I just put it in print. Here, I'll put it in larger type for you:

In a very specialized way, customers are *stupid*.

Now, don't assume you know what I mean by that. Let's trot out one more example for this chapter.

If you've spent any amount of time around a two-year-old, it didn't take long to realize that they are capable of doing anything at any given moment. You can't assume "Oh, they won't stick their head in the toilet and flush until they pass out," you have to watch to make sure they don't, and then tell them not to do that. However, if you do only that...tell them...then they probably won't understand. You have to show them the toilet, and tell them "Don't do that!"

The key point of this example is this: If you just tell them, possibly in the living room while watching "Oprah," they'll smile, nod and agree. You won't see any outward signs at all that they didn't get the message.

Your customers are the same as that two-year-old.

Don't tell them anything; *show* them why you're important to their life, and show them how their life will be better if they listen to you, and give you their business.

Another interesting point; don't assume that showing them

once will get the message through. It'll take a few times before that two-year-old stops giving themselves a "Tid-E-Bowl Blue" scalp, even if you show them every time they do.

Show them, show them often, and never assume they understand what you mean. This applies to two-year-olds...and your marketing.

"Never make a move without commitment."
-David Sandler

Chapter Five:
The Funnel of Love

How do you take your customers from "interested" to "buying"? If you said anything at all about customer service, or deep discounts, or fantastic selection, go back and start the book over. I'll wait until you catch up.

...

Now that everyone's hopefully up to speed, let's talk about your sales funnel, or your lack of one. A sales funnel is exactly that; a device to take a large input and direct it into a smaller opening. In this case, the "large input" is the general public, while the "smaller opening" is labeled "people that will give me money!"

However, just like a physical funnel, your sales funnel must lead the public through different steps; these steps should serve to narrow the group you're dealing with until you reach "people that gave me money!"

The first step in your funnel is advertising. What kind? *Any* kind.

- Flyers

- Door hangers

- Direct mail

- Radio

- Television

- Billboards

- Business cards

- Online advertising

- Word of mouth

Anything that makes someone aware of your business and what you do (hopefully thanks to your USP and/or elevator pitch!) is advertising, and it should have one purpose.

All advertising should lead people to enter your sales funnel.

However, a good sales funnel should do more than just lead people from "Who are you?" to "Here's my check!" Your sales funnel should do all of the following:

- Collect a list of contact information of prospective customers

- Collect a separate list of actual customers

- Create the desire in your customer to move further into the sales funnel

- Provide *opportunities* to move further into the sales funnel

- Provide opportunities for continued marketing to those that spend money with you.

Your sales funnel should have a method to gather the means to continue to market to everyone that enters it, whether they make a purchase or not. In fact, you'll want to have a method of creating a separate list of those that are proven "buyers", because you will want to market to proven customers in a different way. Let's look at a sample sales funnel.

You advertise for people to stop by your business or website, and offer an incentive for them to do so, with a clear call-to-action. (An incentive could be anything from a free item or service to a discount or contest.)

When they take action and pay you a visit, collect contact information from them as part of the incentive; email is the most cost-effective, but allow them to give you a mailing address or phone number if they don't have email.

Once you have this information, you should contact them within a week or so to simply thank them for stopping by, with no sales pitch.

Follow this with a second contact from you, offering tips, hints or any information of interest to your potential customers. In this email, make them an offer. This can be a small offer, but it should be an offer that prompts people to take action!

Continue to market to this group with regular information,

taking care to not endlessly bombard them with offers and requests for their money.

When someone takes action on an offer you send out, they should be removed from the "prospect" list and placed on a separate contact list, exclusively containing the information of customers that have spent money with you. (At the same time, don't forget to upsell them during or immediately after the purchase process!)

This second list can be extremely valuable if used correctly. These are the people that you know will be interested in spending money for your product or service, because they already have!

Continue to drive a steady stream of potential customers through your advertising, then market to those that take action the first time, while marketing separately to the list of proven

customers (with different messages and offers).

This is an overly-simplified take on a sales funnel, but

hopefully it will show you just how important this can be. A

properly-designed funnel can explode your business.

"There seems to be some perverse human characteristic that likes to make easy things difficult."
                                                  -Warren Buffet

Chapter Six:
Your Most Valuable Customer

This should be an easy answer...who is your most valuable customer? The answer is "your last customer". There are a couple of reasons for this:

- You are one of the most recent expenditures they have, so their experience is still fresh on their mind.

- Word-of-mouth is an extremely powerful form of advertising. Someone that will ignore every radio, television and newspaper ad you pay for will show up at your place of business looking to spend money if someone in their circle of influence tells them how happy they are with you.

- Your previous customers are **proven** to be willing to spend money with you, and are *much more likely* to spend money with you in the future than anyone else.

The interesting thing is, many businesses don't effectively market to their list of previous customers. (I'm not talking about *you*, of course, but for the sake of everyone else let's pretend I am and discuss this for a minute.)

How many of your customers have received a follow-up contact from you after their purchase, just to tell them "thank you for your business" and to remind them to call you with any questions or problems they have? Don't try to sell them anything...just say "thank you"...you'll be selling them quite a bit later on!

This might sound "trite" to you, but...it...works! Don't assume they know you're happy they spent their hard-earned money with you (See Chapter 4), *show them!* And don't assume you built goodwill with them because of your "friendly, knowledgeable staff" and "customer service", because every one of your competitors prides themselves on the same thing. It's important, but it doesn't make you stand out if you're relying on the same things your competitors are.

How many of your competitors send a simple "thank you for your business" card, note, email or call after someone makes a purchase with them? If you said "none," then guess what? You just found a simple competitive advantage you can put to work to differentiate yourself from the rest!

You should give your customers the attention they deserve

after they've left your business (or you've completed your service for them), both in marketing and in customer relations. Give them a case of WFD (Warm Fuzzies Disease), because it's highly contagious! This will accomplish two things:

1. It will cause your customers to look at you not as a good option, but the *only* option in their mind, meaning they will be more likely to spend more money with you in the future.

2. It will turn your previous customers into the best sales and marketing force you've ever seen.

I'm willing to bet you have at least one business that you deal with as a customer that you feel is "the only option." You can't imagine going to anyone else for the service or product they provide. Take a long, hard objective look at how you feel for them, and see if you can figure out why you feel that way.

I'm talking about the kind of relationship where you simply don't care what the price is...they are your go-to option in this area.

I'll give you a hint; there are few documented cases of someone becoming infected with WFD because they were exposed to a low price.

An eagle was sitting on a tree resting, doing nothing. A small rabbit saw the eagle and asked him, "Can I also sit like you and do nothing?"☐ The eagle answered, "Sure , why not."☐So the rabbit sat on the ground below the eagle and rested. All of a sudden, a fox appeared, jumped on the rabbit and ate it. Moral of the story: To be sitting and doing nothing, you must be sitting very, very high up.

Chapter Seven:
You Never Write, You Never Call...

Once someone has shown enough interest in what you have to offer to take action on it, you should follow up with them. This sentence isn't rocket science, nor is it a new idea. However, most businesses don't do a very good job of it.

Your call to action may be to stop by your business, visit your website, or simply call you for more information. And every time someone does, you should collect a method of later contacting *them* as part of the process.

Every. Time.

Admittedly, you're not going to get *everyone's*

information, but if you make the effort to try to get everyone's,

you'll be amazed at your success rate. And then you have a

direct line to market to them, which you should use to not

market to them as much as possible.

I know, that makes no sense...at least, on the surface.

However, you should use collected email addresses, for

example, to build a relationship with your customers beyond

"Buy my stuff!" You already do this in your day-to-day

business, you just don't think of it that way.

- Do you greet your customers when they enter your

  business?

- Do you "small talk" with your customers, asking how

51

they're doing, how their day is, or talking about the weather?

- Do you answer their questions and give them advice?

All of these activities are done to help build a relationship with your customer so that they will be more likely to spend money with you. The same exact methods apply to your marketing, too.

Once your collect their email, make sure they get a "Welcome and Thanks!" email first thing, welcoming them to your list of contacts and thanking them for signing up. Don't try to sell them anything. Then, they should get regular emails from you, talking about things that have happened in your business or your community, offering them advice, answering their questions, giving them tips...in other words, building value.

If they look forward to receiving your emails, they will be opened, and they will be read. And then, you can use the opportunity to tell them about your latest special, or a great one-time deal, or the newest thing you have on the shelves, or a great service you provide, or...you get the idea.

Your marketing should follow the same pattern as it does when they walk in your door or call you on the phone. Be helpful, be nice, and don't be pushy, and your sales rate will rise.

And none of that is possible unless you collect a way to contact them.

The best part about this process is the fact that it can be automated using email, cutting your time investment down to practically nothing.

"Advertising people who ignore research are as dangerous as generals who ignore decodes of enemy signals."
-David Oglivy

Chapter Eight:
Follow the tracks, Kemosabe

What's the most effective method of advertising you use for your business? Radio, newspaper, billboards...every business owner has an answer to this question, but few can tell you why.

Most business owners wouldn't dream of using assumptions or personal preferences to determine what inventory to keep on hand, how to establish their pricing or how much insurance to carry on their business, but they have no problem "flying by the seat of their pants" when it comes to spending their advertising dollars.

"Billboards are the most effective advertising I do!"

Okay, great! How do you know that? More often than not, that question will be answered with "I just do!" or "I can see the results!" or, the time-honored classic "I ask my customers!"

Hopefully, the first two answers are self-evident bull. If you run your business using the principle of "I just know how to do it," you've got bigger problems than marketing. Let's put your marketing into perspective:

Marketing is spending money and time to increase your sales.

The most important fact you can know about your marketing is the same as it is for deciding what services to provide, what products to sell or even whether or not to pay a salary to hire addition help...you look at the ROI, or Return On

Investment.

"Whoa, Dave, how the heck am I supposed to do *that*!?" It's easier than you think, as long as you track your advertising. This means you should be able to tell exactly how many customers you get from any marketing activity. For online marketing, that's fairly simple, but the mystery most can't solve is how to track those radio, newspaper and billboard ads. There are several methods you can use:

- Special numbers – This one is fairly foolproof. For every different marketing method you use, set up a special toll-free number that will only appear in that medium. A separate number for billboards, a different one for newspaper. (This can be done for about $4 per month per number.) Then, every time someone calls your "billboard number," you know it was a direct result of your billboard advertising.

- Discount codes – Coupons can do a good job of telling you the effectiveness of your print advertising, but it's hard to ask people to cut out a billboard and bring it in for a discount, or rip your radio commercial out of the dashboard and show it at checkout for a free gift. The answer to this is "gift codes". You've seen these..."mention the word 'rutabaga" and get a free bobblehead!" In newspaper, the word is "rutabaga," while on the radio you're told to mention "kumquat," and their billboards advertise that free bobblehead if you use the word "zucchini". A key point, however...using this method, you must be advertising the same offer in all methods! You have to "compare apples to apples"; if you're offering that bobblehead with the word "rutabaga," and offering a 10 percent discount with the word "kumquat," you don't know if the results you see will show you which marketing method gives you the best ROI, or which offer is more attractive to your market.

• The customer survey – This is not a very effective method. An interesting case study for you: A furniture store owner had been advertising in the local newspaper for a couple of years, then decided to start a radio campaign. After a week or so, he decided that radio just "didn't work for him," and wanted to stop. I came up with this idea for him; stop your newspaper advertising for a week, and during that week run a special deal in a radio campaign only...in other words, the only way for anyone to find out about it would be through radio. Just for fun, I told him to be sure to ask everyone that came in and asked for the deal how they heard about it.

Sixy-eight percent said they had seen it "in the paper", and only two people said they had "heard it on the radio".

Ask them all you want, but they have absolutely no interest in your marketing plan; they will tell you the first thing they think of, which may or may not be true. You can't depend on your customers to track themselves.

"Customers are not on-off switches, but volume dials"
-Don Peppers & Martha Rogers, in The One to One Future

Chapter Nine:
You Get As Good As You Give

You have a proven list of potential customers in your possession right now. This list has a 100% conversion rate. I'll say that again...*a one hundred percent conversion rate.*

That 100% conversion rate list is...your list of current and previous customers.

You know they'll spend money with you, because *they already have.* The question is...are you marketing specifically to them, with targeted messages designed just for that segment of your potential clientèle? If you think that your general marketing message is doing that job, think again. To maximize the potential of your previous customers, you should offer them an incentive to return to your business and spend more money (which *is* the name of the game here).

This can be as simple or as complicated as you want it to be. A nationally-known sandwich shop chain used a fairly simple method for years. When you purchased a sandwich from them, you were issued a business card sized coupon, and had one section punched out at the bottom. When your card was completely punched out (after five purchases) you received a free sandwich.

This may sound like a stupid thing to do. "Give away what I'm selling? Have you lost your mind, Dave?" Not at all. But remember the Golden Rule here: Do unto others as you would have them do unto you.

Want your previous customers to give *you* something (repeat business)? Give your previous customers something *first* (an incentive). Once you do that, you'll invoke the law of reciprocity. I know, I know...big word. What it means is that, when you do something nice for someone, they feel a sense of moral obligation to do something nice for you in return, even if it's as simple as "listen to your offer".

It could be an exclusive discount for former customers, a free t-shirt, a free product or consulatation...all that matters is that it has value to your customers, and you give it with no strings attached.

"You catch more flies with honey than with vinegar," my grandmother used to say, and she was right. Giving your current customers a tangible reason to spend even more money with you is a great example of this, rather than using the

"vinegar" of repeated marketing messages asking for their

money.

Which would stand out to you: yet another flier with a

"Break the Bank!!!" special on your product or service from

your competitor, along with a 20% off coupon...or a certificate

for a FREE sample of that product or service with no purchase

necessary from you? I know which one I would respond to first.

"I have as much authority as the Pope, I just don't have as many people who believe it."

-George Carlin

Chapter Ten:
Why Should Anyone Listen To YOU?

Everyone knows an authority on a subject. For example, if you had a question about your dog, who would you call? Chances are, the name of a friend or acquaintance just popped into your mind. If you're not a pet person, try this one: you need to know something about NFL football (or Major League Baseball, or the NBA, etc)...who do you call?

There are people that become branded as authorities without even trying, because they are known as one of the most knowledgeable people in their area on a subject. They achieved that status by answering questions over the years and providing help to people that were looking for it in their area of expertise. And as a result, their opinion on their topic carries more weight than the opinion of someone who is not considered an authority. They become the "Go-to guy" (or "gal") when you need help.

The interesting thing is this; to set out to become an authority in your field, it doesn't matter if you've been working at it for years or decades. All that matters is how you brand yourself.

By branding, I don't mean renting a billboard on the main highway with your picture and a caption that says "He's the authority!" Like most other things in business, what you *do* counts for much more than what you *say*.

There are some fairly simple things you can do that will lead others to view you as an authority in your field:

- **Write a book** – This sounds harder than it is. If you absolutely stink at writing, get a recorder and talk about what you do. Get it transcribed, and guess what? You have a book. And you also have the ability to tell everyone about it. "Published author" after your name will go a long way toward cementing your reputation as an authority in your field.

- **Public speaking** – Check with your local civic clubs...Rotary, the Exchange Club, the Lions Club...who are always looking for someone to speak at their meetings. There's nothing like giving a twenty minute talk on what you do to a room full of local business owners to expand your image.

- **Set up and advertise a "Troubleshooting Hotline"** - Answering questions about your topic (and letting it be known that you do this) will cause an interesting effect in the public. If you're putting yourself out there as a troubleshooter in your field, people will subconsciously assume you know your stuff. It will also imply that there are problems in your field, and that you know how to solve them.

- **Hold a free seminar** – This is dependent on your business, but most businesses could hold a free seminar on a topic from their field and do well. A pet store owner could give a seminar on "Proper care and feeding of your pet," an accountant could hold a seminar on "Getting Ready for Tax Season," and a plumber could present a seminar on "Simple Fixes for Simple Leaks". If you don't think you have a topic that would work for you, go to the experts...ask your customers what annoys them the most, and then solve it for them.

When your potential customers have a question dealing with whatever business you're in, you want their first thought to be "I know who I need to call!" Make it to this point, and your uphill marketing battle just became a lot less steep.

Afterword

I realize that some of the concepts covered in this book seem "old hat" to some, but there are plenty out there that don't know about them...or, at least, don't put them to use in their daily business life.

My hope is that I've introduced you to a new way of looking at your marketing process. It's possible I made you aware that you should *have* a marketing process. No matter the case, there's one thing to remember:

All that matters is that you're improving. Where you're headed is much more important than where you've been.

If you have any questions at all, feel free to email me at dave@davehughesconsulting.com, and I'll do my very best to answer them for you.